T0372582

British English

Caroline Nixon &
Michael Tomlinson

CAMBRIDGE

Pupil's Book
with eBook

3

Language summary

		Key vocabulary	Key language	Sounds and spelling

Hello!

Simon

Stella

Suzy

 1 🎧 2 **Read and say the name. Listen and check.**

a Hello. I'm nine. I've got a brother and a sister. This is my favourite computer game. It's called 'Brainbox'.

b Hello. I'm five. I've got a big dog. She's black and white and she's called Dotty.

c Hi. I'm eight. I like reading comics. My favourite comic's called 'Lock and Key'.

 2 📝 **Ask and answer. Write.**

What's your name?

My name's …

My name's Zak. I'm nine.

1 What's your name?
2 How old are you?
3 Have you got a brother or a sister?
4 What's your favourite toy called?

LOOK

My favourite comic's **called** 'Lock and Key'.

🎧 3 **Listen and say the number and the colour.**

H-E-L-M-E-T

Helmet. That's number 18 and it's pink and green.

 Play the game.

B-I-K-E

Bike. That's number 17 and it's purple.

 Read and answer.

Computer.

1 It's on the table, next to the books.
2 It's on the box, next to the ball.
3 It's on the floor, in front of the train.
4 It's under the table.
5 It's on the floor, between the helicopter and the monster.
6 It's behind the bike.

Vocabulary: numbers, colours and toys | **Language:** prepositions of place

Read and match the names.

Meera – c

> SCHOOL

> Simon and Stella are in the playground with their friends, Alex , Lenny and Meera , and their sister Suzy. Meera's sitting next to Stella and Simon's talking to Lenny. Alex is behind them.

> DETECTIVE BOX

2 🎧 4 **Listen. Who is it?**

She's drinking orange juice.

That's Meera.

3 **Answer the questions.**

1 What's Stella doing?   She's reading.
2 What's Alex doing?
3 What's Lenny eating?
4 What's Suzy doing?

5 What's Meera drinking?
6 What's Simon doing?
7 What's Alex kicking?
8 What's Stella reading?

STUDY

What**'s** Suzy doing?   What **is** Suzy doing?
She**'s** jumping.   She **is** jumping.

6   **Language:** prepositions of place and present continuous

1 🎵🎧 5 ▶ Listen and say the name.

I've got an old bike
And I'm riding it.
He's got a big kite
And he's flying it.
She's got a small car
And she's driving it.
We've got toys!

I've got a fat doll
And it's talking.
He's got a robot
And it's walking.
She's got a new ball
And it's bouncing.
We've got toys!

2 🎵🎧 6 ▶ Listen and sing. Do karaoke.

3 Read and complete.

1 Yasmin's holding a fat doll.
2 Fred's _____ an old bike.
3 Max is _____ a big kite.

4 Vicky's _____ a small car.
5 Anna's _____ a new ball.
6 Paul's _____ with a robot.

Lock's sounds and spelling

1 🎧 7 ▶ **Watch the video. Watch again and practise.**

2 **Find the sounds and draw a circle or a triangle. Say.**

The spiders ride, fly and drive from nine to five.
They play and paint from eight to late.

3 **Work in pairs. Play, ask and answer.**

What have you got?

What are you doing?

Can you ride a bike?

No, I can't.

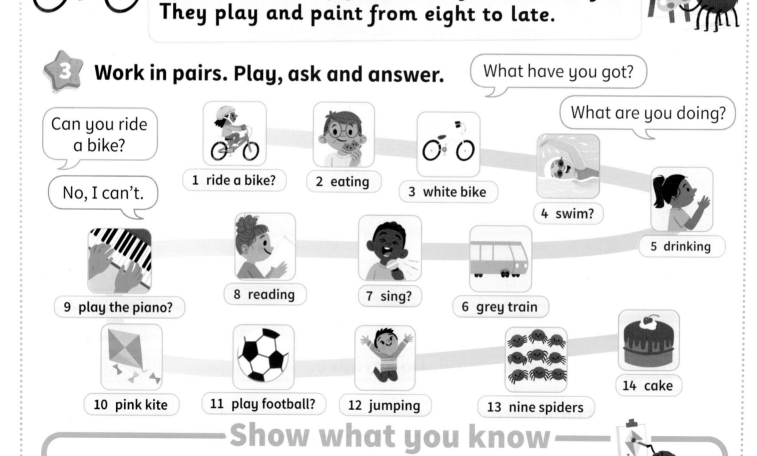

1 ride a bike?

2 eating

3 white bike

4 swim?

5 drinking

9 play the piano?

8 reading

7 sing?

6 grey train

10 pink kite

11 play football?

12 jumping

13 nine spiders

14 cake

Show what you know

The _____ paints a _____ kite.

Sounds and spelling: *i–e, y, ay, ai, ei, a–e, ey*

Lock & Key!

1 Describe the pictures in pairs.

1 Family matters

Family Tree

grandparents

uncle · parents

Grandpa · Grandma

aunt

Uncle Fred · Mrs Star · Mr Star · Aunt May

My family tree.

Stella · Simon · Suzy

daughter/granddaughter · son/grandson · daughter/granddaughter

---

1   9 **Look, think and answer. Listen and check.**

1 Is Stella at school?
2 Who's on the poster?

3 Has Stella got a brother?
4 How many sisters has she got?

2 **Ask and answer.**

1 Who's Stella's uncle? — Uncle Fred.
2 Who's Suzy's aunt?
3 Who are Simon's grandparents?
4 Who are Mrs Star's daughters?
5 Who's Mr Star's son?
6 Who's Grandpa Star's grandson?

LOOK

Who's Stella**'s** uncle?
Who's Suzy**'s** aunt?

3 **Choose and describe. Write.**

My aunt is tall. She's got black hair.

1 🎧 10 **Listen and say the letter.**

He's taking a photo of his son.

Letter e.

2 🎧 11 **Listen and complete.**

Suzy's sitting next to her …

… mum.

3 **Ask and answer.**

Who's playing a game with her aunt?

Stella!

STUDY

He**'s** tak**ing** a photo.
She**'s** paint**ing**.
They**'re** read**ing**.

Language: present continuous   **11**

Look and say the name.

1 Who likes riding bikes?

2 Who likes painting?

3 Who likes reading?

4 Who doesn't like having a bath?

 Read and check.

Hi! I'm Aunt May.

Look at everyone in the garden! Stella's reading. She enjoys reading about science. She's clever and she wants to be a doctor. Simon's wearing his helmet because he's riding his bike. He's with his Uncle Fred. They love riding bikes.

Suzy wants to wash her dog. Dotty's naughty. She doesn't like having a bath. Grandpa's laughing and he's giving Suzy a towel. Suzy needs a towel!

Grandma's quiet. She enjoys painting. She's painting a beautiful picture of her granddaughter, Stella.

 Say 'yes' or 'no'.   No.

1 Simon doesn't enjoy riding his bike.

2 Stella enjoys reading about science.

3 Simon doesn't wear a helmet.

4 Suzy wants to wash her doll.

5 Dotty likes having a bath.

6 Grandma enjoys painting.

 LOOK

Simon enjoys **riding** his bike.

Simon wants **to ride** his bike.

 **Read and complete with a name. Listen and check.**

Aunt May's a doctor,
She's got straight black hair.
¹ Uncle Fred 's a farmer,
His beard is short and fair.
²   is quiet,
She wants to paint all day.
³   is funny,
And his curly hair is grey.
⁴   can be naughty,
He loves 'Lock and Key'.
His sister ⁵   's clever,
And she doesn't like TV.
⁶   isn't quiet,
But she's very small.
Here's our family,
We really love them all.
We really love them all.

 Listen and sing. Do karaoke.

**Draw your family tree.
Talk about your family.**

STUDY

| She's | my | aunt. grandmother. |
| He's | | uncle. grandfather. |

| She's | my | mother's grandmother's | daughter. sister. |
| He's | | father's grandfather's | son. brother. |

Vocabulary: appearance | Language: possessive 's   **13**

Lock's sounds and spelling

 1 🎧 14 ▶ **Watch the video. Watch again and practise.**

 2 **Find and underline the _er_ sounds.**

> Bread, butter, burgers – what's for dinner?
> Father, mother, brother and sister love making dinner.

 3 **Work in pairs. Describe and say 'yes' or 'no'.**

The mother is holding a flower.

No, the mother is eating a burger.

Show what you know

What's for _____ ? It's a _____ .

1 **Are Lock and Key good detectives? Why? Why not?**

How big is your family?

1 🎧 16 **Listen and read. How many cousins has Sofia got? How many have you got?**

My name's Sofia. This is my family. There are 11 people in my family. That's me in the middle with my dad, my mum, my brother Felipe, and Baby Elias.

On the left, you can see Uncle Victor, Grandma and Aunt Fernanda.
On the right, you can see my adult cousins Raquel and Raul, and Raul's wife, Alicia.

How old am I? Eight years old

How tall is Uncle Victor? 183 cm

How tall is Grandma? 163 cm

How old is Felipe? Seven years old

How long is Dad's moustache? 5 cm

How long is Baby Elias's foot? 6 cm

How long is Mum's foot? 24 cm

2 **Use Sofia's poster to answer the questions.**

1 How many adults are there? _____8_____

2 How many children are there? _____

3 Uncle Victor is 183 cm tall. Grandma is 163 cm tall. What's the difference?
_____ cm

4 How many fingers and toes have Felipe, Sofia and Elias got in total?
_____ fingers and toes

5 How many feet are there in the family? _____ feet

6 Sofia's family are going to a restaurant. Four people can sit at each table.
How many tables do they need? _____ tables

3 **When do you use maths in real life? Think and say.**

I count my coloured pencils.

I share sweets with my friends.

DIDYOUKNOW...?
Counting is the oldest form of maths. Humans have been counting for 35,000 years!

Maths: measuring | critical thinking

4 17 **Look at the chart. Listen and write the symbol.**

			Maths function	Symbol	Words
a 15	>	12	Addition	+	plus
b 6	___ 2	= 3	Subtraction	-	minus
c 16	___ 19		Multiplication	x	times
d 10	___ 10	= 20	Division	÷	divided by
e 25	___ 8	= 17		=	equals
f 3	___ 2	= 6		>	is greater than
				<	is less than

5 **Guess and measure. Complete the table.**

	Guess!	Measure!
How tall am I?	___ cm	___ cm
How long is my foot?	___ cm	___ cm
How wide is my hand?	___ cm	___ cm
How wide is my English book?	___ cm	___ cm
How long is my hair?	___ cm	___ cm

6 **Survey and measure your classmates. Complete the table in your notebook. Make greater/less than sentences.**

Ready to write:

Go to Activity Book page 16.

Name	Age	How tall ...?

Jackie is 12. Megan is 11.

12 is greater than 11. 12 > 11.

Project

145 cm

185 cm

85 cm

Make a family numbers poster.

2 Home sweet home

upstairs

lift

stairs

balcony

downstairs

basement

A flat in the town

A house in the village

  Look, think and answer. Listen and check.

1 What buildings can you see?
2 What's in the room under the house?
3 Where's the flat?
4 Has the flat got a garden?

 Describe your house or flat. Then write.

My house is in the village. It has got a kitchen downstairs.

My house is in the city. It has got a balcony.

  Listen and say the letter.

A basement

Letter d.

a

b

c

d

e

f

g

1 🎵🎧 **20** ▶ **Listen and order.** 1 – c

a
Upstairs, downstairs,
One floor or two.
We live here,
What about you?

b
Home is home …,
In a city or a village,
In a house or a flat.
Home is home!
It's where it's at.

c
We've got a basement
Under the floor.
It's got brown stairs
And a purple door.

d
I've got a lift,
It goes up and down.
From my balcony,
I can see the town.

2 🎵🎧 **21** ▶ **Listen and sing. Do karaoke.**

3 **Spot the difference.**

This home's got a balcony.

This home hasn't got a balcony.

1 ▶ **Look, read and match.**

1 – f

Meera moves to a new flat

1 Today Meera and her family are moving. Two workers are carrying the wardrobe to the lorry.

4 Meera's helping. She's taking a lamp upstairs. She's smiling because she can go in the lift.

2 Her new address is 14 Park Road. It's a flat. It's amazing!

5 The workers can't take the big wardrobe in the small lift. They need to carry it up the stairs. It's difficult to carry.

3 Meera and her dad are helping the cleaner to clean the flat.

6 Now they are sitting on the wardrobe. They're having a break. They need a drink.

2 **Write some words to complete the sentences about the story. You can use 1, 2 or 3 words.**

1 Meera and her family ___are moving___ today.

2 The workers can't put the wardrobe in _____ .

3 Meera, her dad and the cleaner _____ her amazing new flat.

4 Meera's carrying a _____ in the lift.

5 The workers need to carry _____ upstairs because the lift is very small.

6 The workers are _____ because they are hot, tired and thirsty.

1 🎧 22 **Listen and say.**

2 🎧 23 **Listen and write the names. Say.**

> May lives at number 72.

> That's pink.

23

37

100

59

64

72

85

98

May

3 **Ask and answer.**

> What number's the yellow door?

> It's number 23.

4 **Talk about where you live.**

> What's your address?

> It's 72 Station Road.

LOOK

thir**teen** – thir**ty**
four**teen** – for**ty**
fif**teen** – fif**ty**
six**teen** – six**ty**
seven**teen** – seven**ty**
eigh**teen** – eigh**ty**
nine**teen** – nine**ty**
a **hun**dred

1 🎧 24 ▶ **Watch the video. Watch again and practise.**

2 **Look and find. Read and underline the sounds.**

See the street where we meet.

Bees at number three and sheep at number thirteen.

Green trees in between.

3 **Work in pairs. Write and say. Listen and complete.**

The house is number 13. My number 13 is blue.

13   14   15   30   40   50

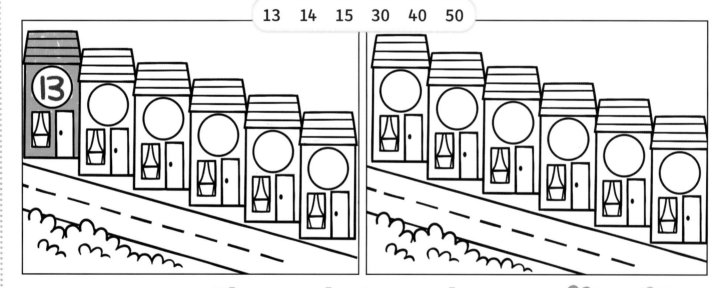

Show what you know

There are _____ bees in the _____ .

1 What does Mrs Potts think about the monster? Say two things.

▶ How are our homes unique?

1 🎧 26 **Listen and read. Which is your favourite home? Why?**

These **cabins** in Norway are on **stilts**, so they don't get wet.

These **flats** in Singapore have got colourful **spiral staircases**.

This **cave home** is in Turkey. It's very old!

Can you imagine living on a traditional Indian **houseboat**? This house can float!

This **tree house** in the USA has got a **rope bridge**.

2 **Write the words from Activity 1 to complete the chart.**

Types of homes	Features
cabin	

3 **What are the advantages and disadvantages of the homes in Activity 1? Think and say.**

It's in a city with shops and transport.

It's very cold / hot.

DID**YOU**KNOW…?
Some cave homes are more than 2,000 years old!

Geography: different types of home | 🛡 critical thinking

4 Read the description of Bethany's dream bedroom. Which parts do you like the most?

My dream bedroom

In my dream bedroom, there's a big bed. I can jump on it! I've got a lot of toys. There's a slide too. It's fast! The walls of my dream bedroom are blue. It's my favourite colour! There's a spiral staircase too. At the top, there's a special bed for my pet cat.

5 Underline the contractions in Activity 4.

Ready to write:

Go to Activity Book page 24.

Learning to write:

Contractions

A contraction is a short form of two or more words. All contractions have an apostrophe (').

there is → there's
it is → it's
I have → I've

6 You are designing your own dream bedroom. Which colours and what things do you want? Think and say.

Project

Design your own dream bedroom.

Review 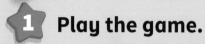 Units 1 and 2

1 Play the game.

Instructions

Lifts – Go up

Stairs – Go down

Pictures – Spell the words. If it's right, roll again. If it's wrong, stop.

2 Look, read and answer.

1 What are the men doing?
2 What's the woman doing?
3 Which room are the family in?
4 What's the boy reading?
5 What's the girl carrying?

3 Look at the pictures. Say which is different.

> Picture d is different. She's got short hair.

Quiz

1 What's Stella's uncle's name? (p10)

2 What are Stella and her aunt doing? (p11)

3 What does Simon's grandmother love doing? (p12)

4 Where can you find a basement? (p19)

5 What are the workers carrying to Meera's new flat? (p20)

6 Say these numbers: 30 – 16 – 13 – 50 (p22)

7 Does Key want to look for Mrs Potts' monster? (p23)

8 Why do some cabins have stilts? (p24)

1 🎧 27 Listen and say the letter. Match.

catch the bus ☐   do homework ☐   get dressed ☐   get undressed ☐
get up ☐   go to bed ☐   have a shower ☐   put on ☐
wake up [a]   take off ☐   wash ☐

 2 Read and complete.

1 Stella ___wakes up___ at seven o'clock every day.
2 Before breakfast she _____.
3 Then she gets dressed and puts on her _____ and leggings.
4 After school Stella does her _____.
5 She washes her _____ before dinner.
6 She _____ and takes off her T-shirt and leggings.
7 Stella goes to bed _____ nine o'clock.

 3 🎧 28 Listen and do the actions.

LOOK

She wakes up at **seven o'clock**.

At **eight o'clock** she catches the bus.

1 🎵🎧 29 ▶ Listen and match.

1 – b

I wake up in the morning,
I get up for breakfast,
I have a shower and I get dressed … **1**
Oooh yes, every day.

I catch the bus
to take me to school …
I do my homework on the way … **2**
Oooh yes, every day.

Lessons start and
I see my teacher … **3**
Eleven o'clock and we're out to play … **4**
Oooh yes, every day.

I wash my hands … **5**
Before I have my dinner …
I get undressed and I go to bed … **6**
Oooh yes, oooh yes,
Oooh yes, every day, every day,
every day.

2 🎵🎧 30 ▶ Listen and sing. Do karaoke.

3 Answer the questions.

He gets dressed at seven o'clock.

1 What time does he get dressed?
2 What time does he do his homework?
3 What time does he start school?
4 What time does he go out to play?
5 What time does he go to bed?

4 Ask and answer.

What do you do before breakfast?

I have a shower.

STUDY

What do you do	before after	breakfast? lunch? dinner? school? bedtime?

1 🎧 31 **Say the chant. Ask and answer.**

> What do you do on Mondays?

> I go swimming.

Monday	Tuesday	Wednesday	Thursday	Friday	Saturday/ Sunday

2 🎧 32 ▶ **Listen and say the day.**

3 🎧 33 **Listen again. Choose the right words.**

1 Simon **always** / **never** plays in the park on Mondays.
2 Simon **always** / **sometimes** does his homework on Mondays.
3 Simon **sometimes** / **never** goes swimming on Wednesdays.
4 Simon **always** / **never** plays in the park on Sundays.

1 Simon never plays in the park on Mondays.

1 Look, read and complete.

James Flunk is a music teacher. At school he ¹ _____always_____ plays the piano but he ² _____ plays the piano in his holidays.

James loves playing tennis, so he ³ _____ plays on Wednesdays. He ⁴ _____ plays football with his daughter Jane, too. She ⁵ _____ scores a goal.

Every Saturday morning James takes his son for his swimming lesson, but James ⁶ _____ goes swimming.

He sometimes takes his family to the mountains on Sundays. They ⁷ _____ sing songs in the car.

2 34 Listen and say 'yes' or 'no'.

3 Look and make sentences. Use the words in the boxes.

I never ride my bike on Wednesdays.

always   sometimes   never

on Saturdays   on Wednesdays
after school   in the morning

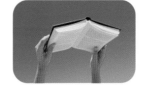

Lock's sounds and spelling

 1 🎧 35 ▶ **Watch the video. Watch again and practise.**

 2 **Find and underline or circle the /IZ/, /z/, and /s/ sounds.**

**Owl dances at night and plays by the moon,
He catches his food and eats before noon.**

 3 **Work in pairs. Write and say.**

The bee flies to the flowers after breakfast.

| fly   dance   get up   go to bed   have a shower   wake up |
| wash hands   eat   brush teeth and hair   sing   do homework |

before breakfast *has a shower*	after lunch	before bed
in the morning	at night	after breakfast
after dinner	before bed	before dinner

Show what you know

The bat _____ and _____ fruit at night.

Lock & Key!

1 Good morning. I'm Johnny Talkalot. On today's show we've got the detectives, Lock and Key, to tell us about their work. We all know detectives work a lot and get up before you and me.

Detective Agency

2 Mr Key, this is Johnny Talkalot. It's nine o'clock! Where are you? You aren't in the detective agency.

Oh no, we never get up before ten o'clock.

3 Everybody knows detectives are very clever.

4 Yes, sometimes we follow people. We're very quiet so they never know we're behind them.

5 YEEOWW! My nose!

6 So, girls and boys, what do you think? Do these detectives work a lot? Are they quiet? And are they very clever?

 Ask and answer the questions in picture 6.

▶ What do astronauts do in space?

Everything floats in space – even our food!

2 🎧 37 **Listen again and tick the true sentences.**

1 There are other astronauts on the Space Station.

2 Sally works on the Space Station.

3 Sally wears a spacesuit.

4 A robot cleaner does the tidying up.

5 Sally watches films in her free time.

3 **Think about the astronaut's day. How is your day similar or different? Think and say.**

I have breakfast, too.

My food doesn't float.

DID YOU KNOW…?
There are no showers on the Space Station, but there are toilets!

4 **Read Sally's blog. What is special about today?**

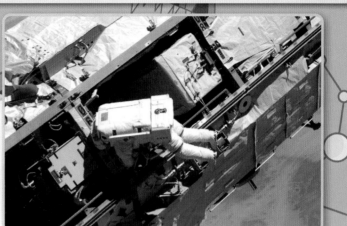

24 June

Today is my first spacewalk. I'm so excited!

I get up at six o'clock and I have a wash.

At half past six, I have breakfast. Eggs and bread! Yum!

Then, I put on my spacesuit. Another astronaut helps me and it takes a long time.

Now it's nine o'clock. The doors open and I go outside. Wow! I've got an amazing view of Earth!

5 **Underline the times in Activity 4.**

Ready to write:

Go to Activity Book page 34.

Learning to write:

Times

six o'clock   half past six   seven o'clock

6 📝 **Prepare for an interview with an astronaut. What questions do you want to ask?**

1 Do you sleep in a bed?

2

Project

Role-play an interview with an astronaut.

Science: astronauts in space | 🛡 communication

35

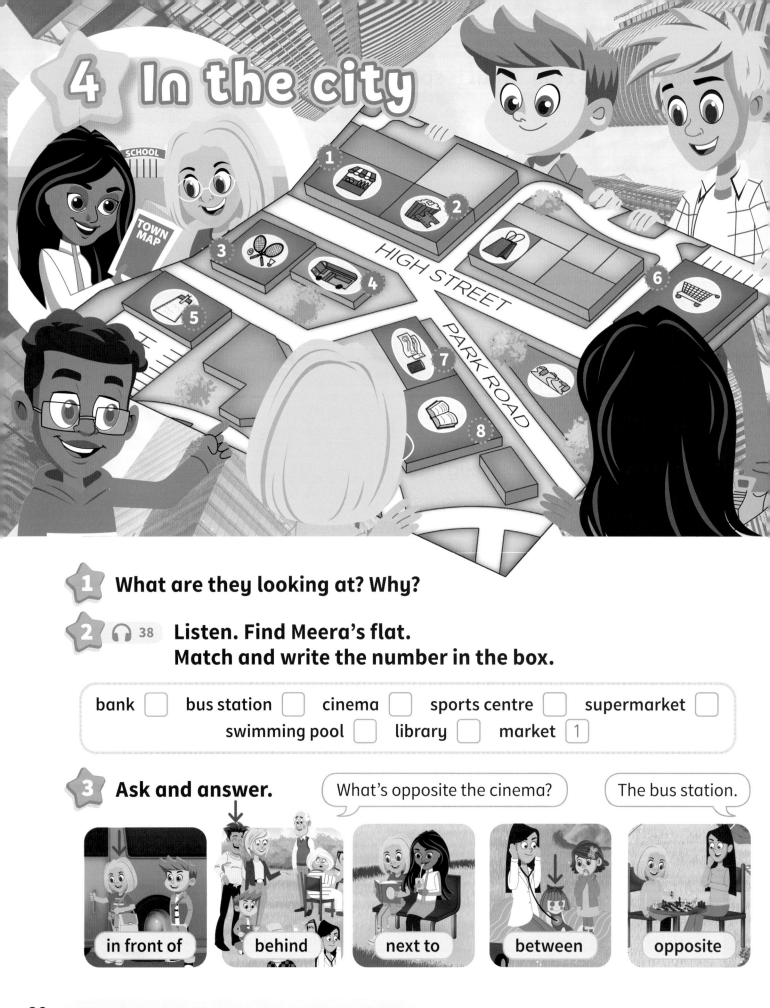

4 In the city

1 What are they looking at? Why?

2 🎧 38 Listen. Find Meera's flat.
Match and write the number in the box.

bank ☐ bus station ☐ cinema ☐ sports centre ☐ supermarket ☐
swimming pool ☐ library ☐ market 1

3 Ask and answer.

What's opposite the cinema?   The bus station.

in front of   behind   next to   between   opposite

Vocabulary: places | Language: prepositions of place

 **1** 🎧 39 **Look at the picture. Listen and answer.**

> Where's the park?

> It's in front of the swimming pool.

2 **Ask and answer.**

> Where's the bin?

> It's in front of the hotel.

3 **Read and complete with words from the picture in Activity 1.**

This is a picture of my town. Look at the ¹ swimming pool opposite the park.
I sometimes go there to swim with Stella. We always take our swimsuits and towels
with us. We go to the ² _____ to buy our food. It's between the bank and the
³ _____. Where do my parents go to get money? They go to the ⁴ _____.
Can you see the ⁵ _____? I go there to catch the bus to school. Where do I love
going on Saturdays? I love going to the ⁶ _____ to see a film. The cinema's my
favourite place in the town. When my grandparents come to town, they stay in
the ⁷ _____.

 **4** 🎧 40 **Listen and answer.**

> Where do you go to see a film?

> I go to the cinema to see a film.

Language: prepositions of place and infinitive of purpose **37**

1 🎧 41 ▶ **Look, think and answer. Listen and check.**

1 Where are the children?
2 Which children are happy?

3 What book has Lenny got?
4 What time is it?

2 🎧 42 **Listen and say 'yes' or 'no'.**

3 **Ask and answer.**

When do you go to the library?   I go to the library on Saturdays.

1 When do you go to the library?
2 What do you enjoy reading?
3 When do you read?
4 Do your family read?
5 Why do you read?

STUDY

Simon **must** be quiet in the library.
They **must** catch the bus.
She **must** do her homework.

1  **Read and match. Listen and check.** 1 – d

1	Must I make my bed, Dad?	Yes, you must.
2	Must I wear a skirt, Dad?	Yes, you must.
3	Must I go to school, Dad?	Yes, you must.
4	Must I do my homework, Dad?	Yes, you must.
5	Must I clean my shoes, Dad?	Yes, you must.
6	Can I play in the park, Dad?	Yes, you can!

2  **Listen and sing. Do karaoke.**

3 **Ask and answer.**

make the bed   clean your room
clean your shoes   help in the kitchen
wash the car   help Mum and Dad

What must you do at home?

I must clean my room.

Lock's sounds and spelling

1 🎧 45 ▶ **Watch the video. Watch again and practise.**

2 **Find and circle the sounds. Say.**

> Where's the bear with purple hair?
> He's over there, on the chair!

3 **Draw lines. Then ask, answer and draw.**

 Where's the small bear?

 The small bear is in the bank.

Show what you know

There's a small _____ with yellow _____ .

Lock & Key!

1 Where must Mrs Potts go? Why? Where must Lock and Key go? Why?

Where do we go shopping?

1 🎧 47 **Listen and read. Which shop is interesting to you? Why?**

Candylawa

Riyadh, Saudi Arabia

Do you like sweets? Candylawa has got it all: sweets, cakes and popcorn. After buying some treats, you can buy nice gifts, such as T-shirts and animal toys. There's also a café for visitors.

Brooklyn Superhero Supply Company

New York City, USA

Are you a superhero? Do you want to be one? This shop has got superhero costumes, such as masks and capes. You can also buy fun toys and science kits to make things! You can build a robot or write a secret message with invisible ink.

2 **Read and match. Then write.**

Brooklyn Superhero Supply Company			What do both shops sell?
	a	in Saudi Arabia	
	b	in the USA	
	c	costumes	
Candylawa	**d**	a café	
	e	sweet treats	

3 **What shops do you like? What do you buy there? Think and say.**

I like craft shops.

I buy paint and crayons.

Why are these shops different? Read and match.

1

MOVING BOOKS

Imagine a van that drives around and sells books! You can buy books in a field or in the car park. Books about space, storybooks, notebooks… you can find them all here!

2

COCONUT DELIGHT

Thirsty? Come and drink some delicious coconut water. You can find us by the beach.

3

C+M ice cream

Can you hear the music? The ice cream van is coming!! It drives to your street or your school and you can buy yummy ice cream.

5 **Underline the nouns in Activity 4.**

Learning to write:

Nouns

A noun is a word for a person, place or thing.

6 **Imagine you want to open a shop. What do you sell? Think and say.**

Ready to write:

Go to Activity Book page 42.

Project

Role-play a conversation at your shop.

Review Units 3 and 4

1 Play the game.

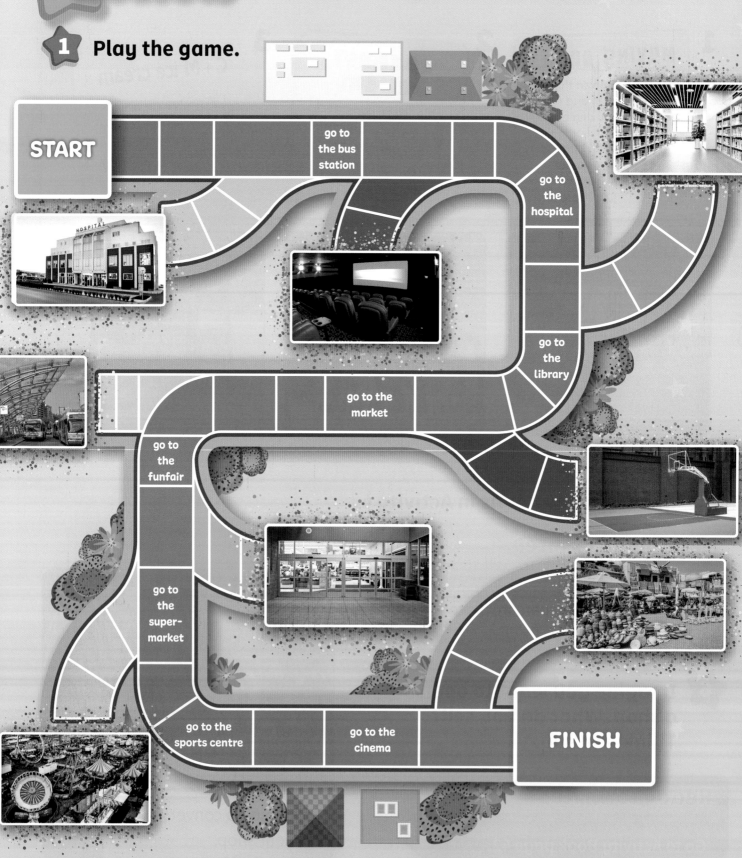

START

go to the bus station

go to the hospital

go to the library

go to the market

go to the funfair

go to the supermarket

go to the sports centre

go to the cinema

FINISH

 **2** 🎧 48 **Listen and choose the correct picture.**

1 What does Jack do on Saturday afternoons?

 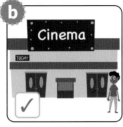 

2 What time does Daisy come home from school?

 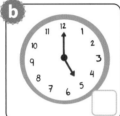 

3 What does Paul do after dinner?

4 Where does Vicky catch the bus?

5 Where's John going?

Quiz

1 What time does Stella catch the bus to school? (p28)

2 What does James Flunk do every Saturday morning? (p31)

3 Do Lock and Key get up before ten o'clock? (p33)

4 Where does Sally work? (p34)

5 On Meera's map, what's opposite the market? (p36)

6 Where do you go to see a film? (p37)

7 Where's the bear with the purple hair? (p40)

8 Why must Mrs Potts and her friend go to the bank? (p41)

5 Fit and well

a temperature   a cold   a cough   a headache   a toothache   a stomach-ache

1 🎧 49 **Look, think and answer. Listen and check.**

1 Where are Stella and Simon?
2 Who's the doctor?
3 Is Stella hot?
4 Is Simon ill?

2 **What's the matter? Act it out.**

What's the matter?

He's got a cough/stomach-ache.

3 🎧 50 **Listen and do the actions.**

STUDY

What's the matter?
He**'s got** a cough.
She**'s got** a temperature.
I**'ve got** a stomach-ache.

Vocabulary: illness | **Language:** *have got* and *has got*

1 🎧 51 Listen and say the letter.

 a
 b
 c
 d

 e
 f
 g
 h

2 Make sentences. Say the letter.

He's She's They've	got	a toothache. a backache. a stomach-ache. a headache.	an earache. a temperature. a cold. a cough.

> She's got an earache.
>
> d

3 Read and say 'yes' or 'no'.

 Poor Stella! Her head hurts and she's very hot. She's got a temperature. She isn't very well because she's got a cough and a bad cold. She must stay in bed and drink lots of water and orange juice. She's sad because she wants to go to school but she can't.

Simon mustn't eat sweets or chocolate today because he says he's got a stomach-ache. Do you think he's got a stomach-ache or do you think he's OK?

1 Stella's back hurts.
2 She's got a temperature.
3 She must stay in bed.
4 She must drink lots of orange juice.
5 Simon says he's got a toothache.
6 He must eat sweets and chocolate today.

4 Work in pairs. Say and guess.

> My stomach hurts.

> You've got a stomach-ache.

 **1** 🎧 52 ▶ **Look, think and answer. Listen and check.**

1 Where's Stella?

2 Who's Mrs Star talking to?

3 What's the matter with Stella?

4 Can she go to school?

2 📝 **Make more sentences.**

> Stella must stay in bed.
> Stella mustn't get up.

3 🎧 53 **Listen and say 'must' or 'mustn't'.**

When you've got a cough you … go out.

mustn't

When you've got a headache you … go to bed.

must

STUDY

You **must** stay in bed.
She **mustn't** go out.

Language: *must* and *mustn't* for obligation

Read the story. Look at the pictures. Write the correct word next to numbers 1–6.

swimming

cough

bed

~~school~~

sleep

doctor

It's Tuesday and Paul's at home. He can't go to ¹ _school_ because he's ill. He's got a temperature. He mustn't get up. He must stay in bed. He's got a ² _____ and a cold. His ³ _____ says he mustn't run or play. He must ⁴ _____ and drink a lot. Paul always has a ⁵ _____ lesson on Tuesdays but he can't go today. He isn't sad because he can listen to music in ⁶ _____!

2 🎵🎧54 ▶ **Listen and move.**

swim

skip

jump

hop

climb

run

dance

Move, move, move.
To be fit and well.
Come on move your body …

Let's have a good time.
Run, swim and climb.
Move, move, move.
Move your body.

Dance, dance, dance.
Don't stop until you drop.
Come on, you know it's fun.

Dance, dance, dance.
Hop, skip and jump.
Come on, you know it's fun.

Let's have a good time …

3 🎵🎧55 ▶ **Listen and sing. Do karaoke.**

🎧 56 ▶ **Watch the video. Watch again and practise.**

 Listen and write.

He's got a cold and he's feeling ill – poor farmer Bill!
The sheep ate all the cake – now they've got a stomach-ache!

 Work in pairs. Describe and say.

She's got a toothache.

She mustn't eat sweets.

Show what you know

_____ ' ___ got a cough and _____ ' ___ got a cold.

Lock & Key!

1 I'm having a big party and I need some detectives to look after my beautiful painting, 'The Toothache'.

No problem, miss Rich.

2 This is my beautiful painting.

Ooh, there are a lot of cakes!

3 There's a lemon cake, a chocolate cake, an apple cake and a carrot cake.

Would you like a cake, Sir?

4 I'd like a lemon cake, please. Which cake would you like, Key?

Er ..., I can't choose. Oooh ... Which cake?

5 Look. I've got an apple cake, I've got a carrot cake, I've got a lemon cake and I've got a chocolate cake.

Oh, Key. That's not good for you.

6 Hmm, what's the matter Key?

I've got some chocolate cake and now I've got a stomach-ache, too.

... and I haven't got my beautiful painting!

1 **How many cakes does Key have? Which cakes are they?**

What remedies do we use?

1 🎧 58 **Listen and read. Do you use any of these remedies? Do you think they work?**

What do you do when you're ill? Here are some common home remedies!

Soup – have you got a cold or the flu? Chicken soup is a famous food remedy. In some countries, lizard soup is popular!

Herbal tea – hot tea is a popular remedy. Herbal teas come from different parts of plants. Have you got a sore throat or stomach-ache? These teas can help you.

Essential oils – essential oils come from plants, too. You can use essential oils on your skin for headaches and muscle aches. But be careful! One or two drops is enough.

REMEMBER! Water's always good for you!

2 **Look and suggest a remedy from the text. Write your answer on the lines.**

1 　**2** 　**3** 　**4**

essential oils

3 **What other home remedies or health advice can you think of? Think and say.**

Take vitamin C.　　Stay in bed.

Put ice on it.

DID YOU KNOW...?
Most remedies come from plants – about 70%!

4 **Read the leaflet. What is the problem? How can you treat it?**

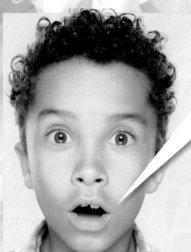

Help!
I've got the
hiccups!

Hiccup facts

Hiccups can happen when you're cold or when you eat too fast.

Hiccups come from muscle movements. They cause you to make a "hiccup" noise. You can't control the hiccups.

How to treat the hiccups

✓ Hold your breath and count to ten.

✓ Eat a spoon of honey or sugar.

✗ Don't worry. Hiccups usually stop after a few minutes.

5 **Underline the imperative verbs in Activity 4.**

Learning to write:

Imperatives

<u>Count</u> to ten. <u>Don't worry</u>.

Ready to write:

Go to Activity Book page 52.

6 **In pairs, give examples of other illnesses. Complete the table in your notebook.**

Illness	Do	Don't
toothache		

Project

Make a class book of remedies.

6 In the countryside

leaf/leave

field

picnic

plant

waterfall

grass

rock

forest

lake

river

 1 🎧 59 **Look, think and answer. Listen and check.**

1 Where do they want to go?
2 Does Mr Star want to play tennis?

3 What does Simon want to do?
4 What does Stella want to do?

 2 🎧 60 **Listen and say the letter.** Forest   Letter e.

 3 **Ask and answer.**   What do you want to do in the countryside?

I want to have a picnic and swim in the river.

1 Read and complete.

A picnic without bread

Charlie and his sister Lily enjoy having picnics in the countryside. Today they're having a picnic in the forest with their grandmother.

Charlie and his grandmother are sitting on a blanket. They're putting the picnic on it. After lunch, Charlie wants to do his homework. He must look at the plants and draw their leaves.

Charlie looks sad because the bread's very old and they can't eat it for lunch …

Lily's standing next to the lake! She looks happy because she's throwing bread to the ducks. It isn't the bread for the ducks, it's the new bread for their picnic.

The ducks are eating the family's lunch!

1 Today Charlie and Lily are eating lunch in …
2 … wants to draw the plants and their leaves.
3 Charlie doesn't like his bread because …
4 Lily isn't sitting … with her brother and grandmother.
5 She's giving the new bread to …
6 The ducks are having … for lunch!

> Today Charlie and Lily are eating lunch in the forest.

 ## 2 Complete the story. Use words from the box.

> countryside ~~picnics~~ old blanket grandmother his very lake eat picnic ducks

Charlie and Lily like going for ¹ _picnics_ in the countryside. Today they are in the ² _____ with their grandmother. Charlie and ³ _____ ⁴ _____ are putting the food on the ⁵ _____ . Charlie's looking at the bread because it's ⁶ _____ , so they can't ⁷ _____ it. Next to the ⁸ _____ , Lily's throwing bread to the ⁹ _____ . It's the nice new bread for the family's ¹⁰ _____ !

1 … puts the table under a tree.
2 … helps Simon.

3 … wants some food.
4 … isn't happy with her drawing.

2 🎧 62 **Close your books. Listen and answer.**

3 **Mime and guess.** (Are you thirsty?) (Yes, I am.)

LOOK

Shall I help you with the blanket?

Yes, please.

1 ♫🎧 63 ▶ **Read and complete. Listen and check.**

bad   hair   long   quiet   tall   ~~thin~~

People, people here or there.
People, people everywhere.
Different colours, different skin.
Bodies that are fat, bodies that are ¹ thin .

Some are weak, some are strong,
With hair that's short or hair that's ²   .
Straight, curly, dark or fair.
Different people, different ³   .

People, different people, different.
Hungry, thirsty, happy or sad,
Young or old, good or ⁴   .
People are big, people are small.
People are short, people are ⁵   .

People, different people, different.
Funny, naughty, angry or tired,
Clever, beautiful, loud or ⁶   .
People, people here or there.
People, people everywhere.

2 ♫🎧 64 ▶ **Listen and sing. Do karaoke.**

3 🎧 65 **Listen and write. Match the words and the pictures.**

1 A-N-G-R-Y   Angry – d

Lock's sounds and spelling

 66 ▶ **Watch the video. Watch again and practise.**

In the forest, parrots sit on the grass by the river. They watch their bread and grapes so crocodiles can't steal their dinner!

2 **Listen and write.**

3 **Look, ask and answer.** (What's the big crocodile doing?) (It's sitting by the river.)

Show what you know

The _____ is swimming in the _____ .

Lock & Key! 6

Describe the pictures. What are they doing?

Why do we live in different places?

1 🎧 68   **Listen and read. Which place do you prefer? Why?**

City: Singapore

Hi! I'm Tara. I'm a teenager and I live in Singapore. I love my city because it's really big and there's lots to do. I live on the 36th floor and from my window I can see shops and the skate park. The city is great, but I think there's a lot of traffic and pollution, and that isn't good for us.

Countryside: Argentina

Hello, I'm Emilio. I live in the countryside in Argentina because my dad's a farm worker. My mum's English and she's a writer. I like my life in the countryside because it's quiet and we've got a big garden with apple trees. I love nature, but sometimes it's a bit boring because I don't meet many people and it's difficult to make friends. All my friends live far away!

2   **Read and put a tick in the correct column.**

	City	Countryside
1 People have got more space to live.		✓
2 The air isn't clean.		
3 There's less noise.		
4 There's more public transport.		
5 People can enjoy nature more.		

3   **What are the advantages and disadvantages of living in the city? Think and say.**

It's very noisy.

Disadvantage!

DIDYOUKNOW...?
Most people in the world live in towns and cities – about 60%!

4 **Read the emails. Underline the advantages of each place in green and the disadvantages in blue.**

Dear Metin,

I'm Ruby, and I'm from Australia. I live in the Outback in a small town called Kemble Creek.

I love living in the countryside because I like riding horses. My horse is called Zara and she loves it when we ride out to visit my aunt. I don't see my friends a lot because they live far away.

Please write soon!

Ruby

Hi Ruby,

I'm Metin. I'm a teenager and I live in Istanbul. It's a huge city with lots to do. I go skateboarding in the park with my friends every day.

I live with my sister, Defne, and my mum. My mum is a builder!

I love the city, but there's a lot of pollution. I don't like that!

Take care,

Metin

5 **Circle the capital letters in names and places in Activity 4.**

Ready to write:

Go to Activity Book page 65.

Learning to write:

Capitalisation

I'm Leo. I live in New York.

6 📝 **In pairs, say advantages and disadvantages of the place where you live. Complete the table in your notebook.**

I live in _____	
Advantages of living here	Disadvantages of living here

Project

Do an interview on life in the city or the countryside.

Review Units 5 and 6

1 Play the game.

START

1

2

3 You mustn't swim in the lake. Go back 2.

4

5 You can cross the bridge. Go forward 2.

6 Your feet are wet. Go back 2.

7

8 It's dark. You must go forward 1.

9

10 You must throw a six and throw again to climb the mountain and continue.

11

12 You can walk in this field. Go forward 2.

13

14

15 There's a forest. You must miss a turn.

16

17

18 You can't find your hat. Go back 2.

19

20 You want to go home. Throw again.

21

22

23

24 You can see the car. Go forward 1.

25

26 You take a photo of a waterfall. Go back 3.

FINISH

Find eight more differences.

In picture 1, there are five bananas. In picture 2, there are four bananas.

 Choose the right words. Say.

chocolate

a field

a river

a temperature

a picnic

a headache

a blanket

1 Cows and sheep sometimes live here.   A field.
2 Fish can swim here.
3 Charlie's got a toothache. He mustn't eat this.
4 This is when your head hurts.
5 You have this when you aren't well and you're very hot.
6 You put this on your bed when you're cold.

Quiz

1 Why must Stella go to bed? (p46)

2 What's the matter with Paul? (p49)

3 What's Miss Rich's beautiful painting called? (p51)

4 What are Lily and her family doing in the forest? (p55)

5 Is Suzy hungry or thirsty? (p56)

6 Where do Lock and Key want to go for a picnic? (p 59)

7 What's an advantage of living in the city? (p60)

8 Where does Ruby live? (p61)

7 World of animals

Animals of the World

bear
whale
panda
lion
dolphin
bat
kangaroo
parrot
shark
jellyfish

 🎧 69 **Look, think and answer. Listen and check.**

1 What are Simon and Stella doing?
2 Which animals are strong?

3 Which animal does Stella like?
4 Which animals talk a lot?

 Ask and answer.

Which animals do you like?

I like pandas.

Where do they live?

They live in the forests and mountains in China.

 🎧 70 **Complete with the words in the box. Listen and check.**

1 Dolphins, jellyfish, whales and sharks live in the ___sea___ .

night   sleep
sea   leaves   meat

2 Bears eat fish, fruit, plants and _____ .
3 Kangaroos eat _____ .
4 Lions are strong and they _____ a lot.
5 Bats sleep in the day and get their food at _____ .

1 Read and match.

1 This huge grey animal lives in the sea. It's got a very big mouth and a lot of teeth. It can sometimes eat people. ☐ e

2 This grey animal lives in the sea. It's got a long nose and small teeth. It's very clever and it likes playing. ☐

3 This big brown animal lives in Australia. It's got two long, strong legs and two short, thin arms. It can jump. ☐

4 This animal can fly. It eats fruit. It can be red, green and blue and it's very loud. ☐

5 This big animal is grey, brown or white. It's big and it can stand on two legs. It eats fish, meat, fruit and plants. It sleeps when it's cold. ☐

6 This black and white bird can swim, but it can't fly. It lives in very cold water and it eats fish. ☐

2 Play the game.

This animal has got a long nose and small teeth.

It's a dolphin.

3 Read and complete with the words in the box.

eats   cold   sometimes   ~~huge~~   grey   sea   animals

This ¹ huge blue or ² _____ animal lives in the ³ _____
It likes very ⁴ _____ water. It ⁵ _____ a lot of small sea
⁶ _____ and plants. It's ⁷ _____ very long.

1 🎧 71 ▶ **Look and answer. Listen and check.**

1 Who's doing a project on animals?
2 Which two animals are they looking at?
3 Can bats carry trees?
4 Are elephants strong?

2 **What do you think?**
Read and say 'yes' or 'no'.

1 Whales are bigger than penguins.
2 Dolphins are longer than whales.
3 Lions are quicker than pandas.
4 Bats are dirtier than elephants.
5 Jellyfish are better at climbing than pandas.
6 Sharks are worse at swimming than kangaroos.

STUDY

Regular:
clean + er – clea**ner**
big + g + er – big**ger**
dirty - y + ier – dirt**ier**
Irregular:
good – **better**
bad – **worse**

1 🎵🎧 72 ▶ **Listen and complete. Sing the song.**

~~bigger~~ see me hiding snake smaller can than

I'm walking,
I'm walking.
What can I see?
I can see a lion and it's ¹ bigger
than me.

I'm swimming,
I'm swimming.
What can I see?
I ² see a shark
and it's uglier ³ me.

I'm standing,
I'm standing.
What can I see?
I can see a ⁴
and it's thinner than me.

I'm hiding,
I'm ⁵ .
What can I see?
I can see a bat
and it's ⁶ than me.

I'm sitting,
I'm sitting.
What can I see?
I can ⁷ a monkey
and it's naughtier than ⁸ .

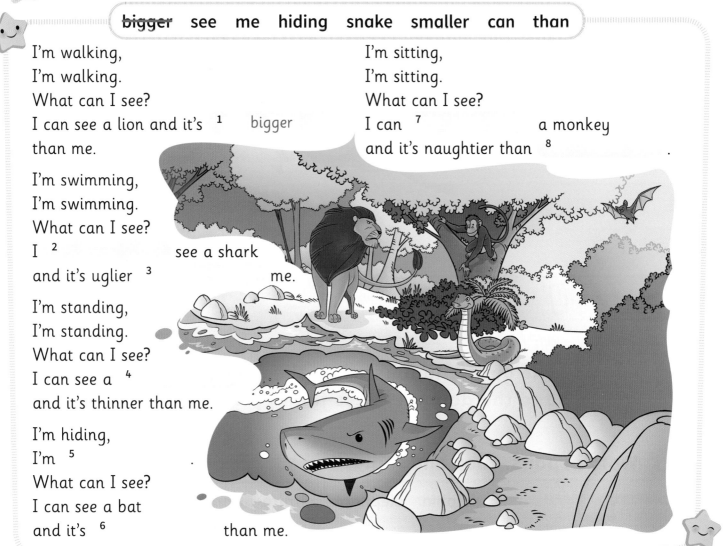

2 🎵🎧 73 ▶ **Listen and sing. Do karaoke.**

3 **Make sentences. Use the words in the boxes.**

The cat's weaker than the lion.

quiet
strong
weak

long
big

fat
slow

bad/good
at jumping

Language: comparative adjectives and present continuous   67

Lock's sounds and spelling

1 🎧 74 ▶ **Watch the video. Watch again and practise.**

2 **Find and underline the sounds.**

> The giraffe laughs when the frog coughs, and the dolphin takes funny photographs!

3 **Work in pairs. Look and say.**

dolphin   elephant   giraffe   frog

coughing   laughing   taking a photo   flying   boat   forest   sea   desert   tree

In the sea, there's a dolphin with a phone.   Number 2!

Show what you know

The _____ takes a _____ of the _____.

 Why does Key think the man isn't Robin Motors? Say 5 things.

How do animals stay safe?

1 🎧 76 **Listen and read. Which animal is bad for birds?**

 Grasshoppers are green, yellow and brown. They use camouflage, so animals can't see them in the grass. They can jump with their big legs to escape from other animals.

 Hummingbirds are very small. They've got bright colours. They can fly very fast, so other animals can't catch them.

 Monarch butterflies have got orange and black wings. They can fly. They're poisonous to birds.

 Sea turtles are green, brown or black. They live in the sea. They can swim. They've got hard shells, so other animals can't eat them.

2 **Read again and complete the chart.**

animal	colours	How do they stay safe?
grasshoppers	green, yellow and 1 _____	use camouflage. They can jump.
monarch 2 _____	orange and 3 _____	They're 4 _____ to birds.
hummingbirds	bright colours	They can fly very 5 _____ .
sea turtles	green, brown or black	They've got hard 6 _____ .

3 **Work in pairs. Say and guess.**

It's got big legs.

A grasshopper!

DIDYOUKNOW...?
Octopuses can change colour to have better camouflage.

4 Read the description of the imaginary animal. What can you say about the animal?

This is a 'hippoctopus.'
It's part hippo, part octopus. It lives in the sea. It's pink and orange. It's got big teeth to scare away sharks.
It eats starfish.
It can swim fast.

5 Circle the adjectives in Activity 4.

Learning to write:

Adjectives
It is <u>pink</u> and <u>orange</u>.
It's got <u>bright</u> colours.

Ready to write:

Go to Activity Book page 70.

6 Combine two animals and invent a name. What features has it got?

It's part zebra, part parrot. It's a zebrot!
It's got the colourful wings of a parrot.

Project

<u>Eleraffe</u>
It's an elephant and a giraffe. It has giraffe legs.

Write a fact file for an imaginary animal.

Dear Meera,
We're on holiday in the countryside.
It's windy and we can fly our kites.
It's very wet too. It's raining now.
It rains every day here!
Simon and Stella

Dear Simon,
I'm on holiday at the beach.
It's hot and sunny! It's very dry here because it isn't raining. Look at me in my swim shorts!
Lenny

Dear Grandma and Grandpa,
We're on holiday at the lakes with Dotty. It's cloudy but I can see a rainbow! It's really beautiful.
Suzy

Dear Stella,
I'm on holiday in the mountains. It's brilliant! It's cold and there's lots of snow. Look at my snowman!
Meera

1 Ask and answer. Look and check.

1 Who's got a pet?
2 Where's Meera on holiday?
3 Who's on holiday in the countryside?
4 Where's Lenny on holiday?

2 Look and say the name.

It's windy.   Simon and Stella!

3 🎧 77 Listen and say 'yes' or 'no'.

1 🎧 78 Listen and match.

1 – snowing

 windy  ☑ snowing  raining  sunny   rainbow  cloudy

2 🎧 79 Listen and complete.

1 It's _____ in the mountains.

2 In the forest it's _____ .

3 It's _____ on the island.

4 It's _____ and _____ at the lake.

5 At the beach it's very _____ .

6 You can see a _____ near the fields.

3 Ask and answer.

What's the weather like at the beach?   It's windy.

Language: *What's the weather like? It's (windy).*   73

1 🎧 80 ▶ **Look, think and answer. Listen and check.**

1 Who's Alex talking to?
2 Who's Alex with?
3 Where's Alex today?
4 Is the weather cold today?

yesterday

today

2 🎧 81 **Listen and say 'yesterday' or 'today'.**

3 **Ask and answer.**

Where were you yesterday evening?

I was at the sports centre.

STUDY

It **was** wet and windy yesterday.
They **were** out yesterday.
It**'s** hot and sunny today.
They **are** at home today.

Language: past simple – *was* and *were*

1 ♫🎧 82 ▶ Read and complete. Listen and check.

coat   cold   hat   scarf   snow   sweater   windy

, coat, sweater and scarf,

It was cold and  in the park, cold and windy …

It was grey and cloudy,

There wasn't any sun,

There weren't many children, it wasn't much fun.

Hat, , sweater and scarf,

It was and windy in the park, cold and windy …

There wasn't a rainbow,

There wasn't any  ,

Grandpa and I were ready to go.

Hat, coat, sweater and  ,

It was cold and windy in the park, cold and windy …

Back at home,

It was much better,

With a hot drink, and my big red  .

 , coat, sweater and scarf,

It was cold and  in the park, cold and windy …

Windy in the park …

2 ♫🎧 83 ▶ Listen and sing. Do karaoke.

3 ⭐ Make sentences.

> It was hot and sunny. He was in a T-shirt and swim shorts.

> It was cold and windy. His gloves were grey and his scarf was blue.

sunny   rainy   snowy   dry   wet   hot   cold   swim shorts   T-shirt   gloves   coat   scarf

Lock's sounds and spelling

1 84 ▶ **Watch the video. Watch again and practise.**

2 📝 **Listen and write.**

> In the sunny sky, bees dance and parrots fly.
> A giraffe's over there sitting on a red chair.
> He watches the bear paint frogs with no hair.

3 **Work in pairs. Say and guess.**

I was in a T-shirt. I was next to a jellyfish in the sea.

You were at the beach. It was sunny and dry!

Show what you know

The _____ paints _____ on a _____ day.

Lock & Key!

8

1

Key! The police have got Robin motors! Let's go to the police station to ask him some questions.

I don't think it was him, Lock.

2

Are you cold, Lock? No problem. We can go in the car.

But we haven't got a car now ... and it's raining!

3

So, mr motors. Where were you last Thursday morning?

Thursday morning? At what time?

At eleven o'clock.

4

You were in Baker Street at eleven o'clock last Thursday morning.

No, I wasn't.

Oh yes you were.

5

YOU WERE IN MY CAR LAST THURSDAY MORNING!

No, mr Lock ... He was here at the police station.

6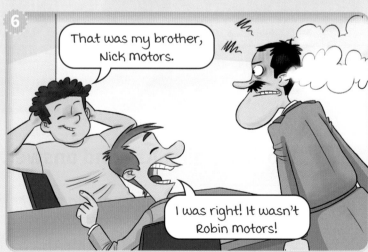

That was my brother, Nick motors.

I was right! It wasn't Robin motors!

1 **Work in pairs. Describe the pictures.**

In picture 1, Lock's happy.

Story: unit language in context   77

What does nature sound like?

1 🎧 86 **Listen. What do the instruments sound like?**

animals   birds   rain   thunder

a    b    c    d

2 🎧 87 **Read and match. Listen and write 'wind' or 'percussion'.**

b Instrument: rain stick

Family of instruments:
percussion
Country: Chile
Sounds like: rain

☐ Instrument: vuvuzela

Family of instruments:

Country: South Africa
Sounds like: elephants

☐ Instrument: thunder drum

Family of instruments:

Country: Indonesia
Sounds like: thunder

☐ Instrument: didgeridoo

Family of instruments:

Country: Australia
Sounds like: Australian birds

3 **Work in pairs. Ask and answer.**

What country is the vuvuzela from?

South Africa.

DID YOU KNOW...?
A sea organ is a musical instrument that you don't need to play. Waves make the music.

4 Read the invitation. What is the event? What do you need to know about it?

You're invited!

Come to our nature sounds concert! You can hear musical instruments that sound like thunder and rain. Make your own instruments, too!

Date: Saturday, 14th May

Time: 4 pm

Place: Kyle's garden

RSVP: Please message us on 0786547112 to let us know you're coming. See you on Saturday!

Kyle and friends

5 Underline the key information with the correct colours.

What? Where? When?

Learning to write:

Key information
What? Where? When?

6 In groups, list musical instruments you have or can make. Who's going to play each instrument?

Name	Instrument

Project

Plan a musical event and make a poster.

Ready to write:

Go to Activity Book page 78.

Review Units 7 and 8

1 Play the game.

Instructions

1 Play in pairs.
2 Choose:
 - weather and clothes
 - animals
 - in town
 - in the countryside
3 Write the topic and the 7 words in your notebook.

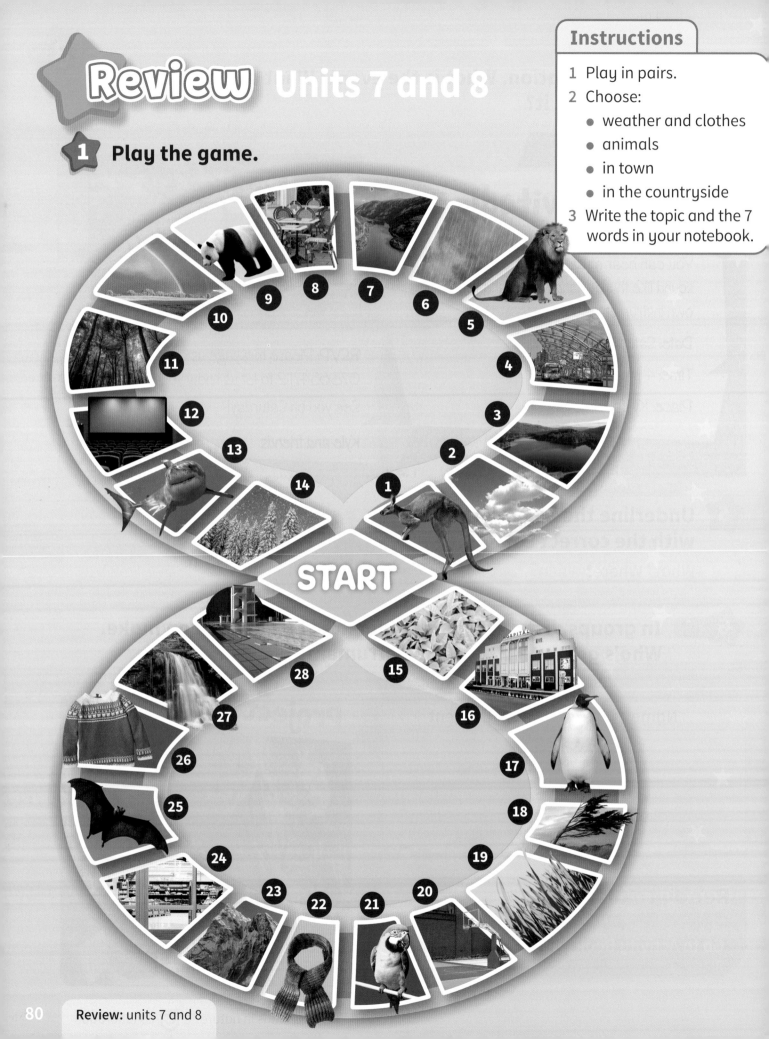

START

Daisy _____   Anna _____   Beth _____

Jack _f_   Abdul _____   Zak _____

Quiz

1 Which 3 animals are in the sea? (p 64)

2 This bird can swim but it can't fly. What is it? (p 65)

3 Where do Lock and Key go for a cold drink? (p 69)

4 Where was Meera on holiday? (p 72)

5 What was the weather like at the park and what was Grandpa wearing? (p 75)

6 Say all the different sounds on page 76.

7 Where was Robin Motors last Thursday morning? (p 77)

8 What instrument is played by the waves in the sea? (p 78)

1 🎧 89 **Look and complete. Listen and check.**

1 The boys' clothes are too _____ .
2 Ana can eat the _____ they planted.
3 The children are painting the _____ .
4 The children are putting _____ into the boxes.

2 **Read and correct.**

1 They share toys with other people.
2 The children are planting flowers in the community garden.
3 The children are painting the wall red.
4 The children are putting the food in the cupboard.
5 The boys want to keep their clothes.
6 One person eats the food from the community garden.

3 **Think and discuss. What do you share?**

I share a computer with my brother.

1 🎧 90 **Look and think. Say 'yes' or 'no'. Listen and check.**

1   In the street, it's OK to throw rubbish on the ground.
2   It's OK to park your car next to a 'No parking' sign.
3   On the train, it's OK not to give your seat to an elderly person who needs to sit down.
4   In a park, it's OK to play football next to the flowers.

 2 **Read and match.**   (1 – b)

1   Don't break flowers …
2   You can put your …
3   You can park …
4   On trains and buses don't …
5   Don't park next to …
6   You can help to make your …

a   … sit in seats that are for elderly people.
b   … and trees in the park.
c   … rubbish in the bin.
d   … town clean and beautiful.
e   … the no parking sign.
f   … in the car park.

 3 **Think and discuss. What can you do to help your town?**

I can have a picnic in the park and put my rubbish in the bin.

1 91 **Look, read and match. Listen and check.**

1 You mustn't be angry when you don't win.

2 In sport you must help other players.

3 In sport it is good to learn new skills.

4 When you play sport you need to know the rules.

2 **Read and correct.**

1 We mustn't be friendly to the other players.

2 You must never follow the rules of the game.

3 When we play sport it's always important to win.

4 Don't help other players.

5 It isn't important to enjoy playing sport.

6 We must be angry when we don't win.

3 **Think and discuss. Is it important to play or to win? Why?**

I think it's important to play, because I can learn new things.

🎧 92 **Look and think. Say 'yes' or 'no'. Listen and check.**

1 If you live near your school you can sometimes walk there.
2 When you clean your teeth you can turn the water off.
3 You mustn't take bags with you when you go shopping.
4 You never need to turn computers or televisions off.

 Read and match.   (1 – d)

1 Turn off the computer when …   a … you can walk there.
2 Don't always use the car, catch …   b … turn off the water.
3 When you clean your teeth, …   c … when you go out of the room.
4 Take bags with you …   d … you aren't using it.
5 Turn off the light …   e … when you go shopping.
6 When you live near your school, …   f … a bus or ride a bike.

 Think and discuss. What can you do to help the world?

I walk or ride my bike to school.

Grammar reference

The doll is next to the ball.
The book is on the floor.
The bike is in front of the table.
The helicopter is under the table.
The game is between the doll and the camera.
The kite is behind the bike.

What are you doing?	I'm riding my bike.
What's Daisy doing?	She's reading.
What's Peter doing?	He's flying a kite.
What are Paul and Jane doing?	They're playing hockey.
Is Pete flying a kite?	Yes, he is. No, he isn't.

Who's Simon?	He's Stella's brother.
Who's Suzy?	She's Stella's sister.
Who are Grandma and Grandpa Star?	They're Stella's grandparents.

I He/She	like / love / enjoy don't like / love / enjoy likes / loves / enjoys doesn't like / love / enjoy	riding my bike. reading about science.
I He/She	want wants	to ride my bike. to read about science.

Do you like taking photos?	Yes, I do.
Do you want to take a photo?	No, I don't.
Does he/she enjoy playing football?	Yes, he/she does.
Does he/she want to play football?	No, he/she doesn't.

Has your house got a basement?	My house hasn't got a basement. My house has got three bedrooms.

What do you do before school? What does he/she do before school?	I have breakfast. He/She has breakfast.
How often do you play in the park? How often does he/she play in the park?	I never / sometimes / always play in the park. I play in the park every day. He/She never / sometimes / always plays in the park. He/She plays in the park every day.

| Where do you go to play basketball? | You go to the sports centre to play basketball. |
| Must I / Simon / Suzy go to school? | Yes, you / he / she must. |

| What's the matter? | I've / You've / He's / She's / We've / They've got a headache. My head hurts. |

He must stay in bed. He mustn't go to the park.
We must be quiet in the library. We mustn't eat in the library.

| I'm hungry. I'm cold. | Shall I make breakfast? Shall I close the window? |

| weak → weaker
thin → thinner
naughty → naughtier
good → better
bad → worse | Parrots are weaker than bears.
Dolphins are thinner than whales.
Monkeys are naughtier than lions.
Sharks are better at swimming than elephants.
Pandas are worse at jumping than kangaroos. |

What's the weather like?		It's sunny.
I / He / She / It You / We / They	was / wasn't were / weren't	at the park yesterday. at the beach yesterday.
Where were you / they on Saturday? Where was he / she / it on Sunday?		
It There There	was / wasn't was / wasn't were / weren't	cold and windy yesterday. a lot of snow yesterday. a lot of children yesterday.

Movers Listening

1 🎧 93 **Describe the pictures. Listen. Circle the correct picture. There is one example.**

2 🎧 94 🐵 **Listen and draw lines. There is one example.**

Clare   Jack   Jim   Fred

Charlie   Sally   Julia

Movers Listening

1 🎧 95 **Listen. Draw the missing information. There is one example.**

  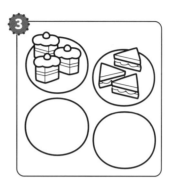 

2 🎧 96 🐵 **Listen and tick (✓) the box. There is one example.**

Example

What is the story about?

A ✓ B ☐ C ☐

1 What is the matter with Clare today?

A ☐ B ☐ C ☐

2 What is Zoe's brother doing?

A ☐ B ☐ C ☐

3 Who is Paul's science teacher?

A ☐ B ☐ C ☐

4 Where were Charlie's socks?

A ☐ B ☐ C ☐

5 What time must Jane get up?

A ☐ B ☐ C ☐

Movers Listening

1 Colour each thing a different colour. Talk to your partner. What's different? Tick (✓).

The flower in front of the tree is yellow.

Mine too!

No, my flower is pink. Let's tick!

blanket ☐	towel ☐	flower ☐	one bird ☐	one cloud ☐	sandwich ☐

2 🎧 97 Listen and colour and write. There is one example.

Movers Reading and Writing

1 Read. Cross out the word. There is one example.

1. a whale
2. a park
3. a market
4. a farm
5. a rainbow
6. a cinema
7. stairs
8. a city
9. breakfast

Chickens often live here.
a farm

You go up and down these
when you're inside a house.

People can go here to buy food.

You sometimes see this
when it's rainy _and_ sunny.

It's a busy place with lots
of people, buses and cars.

People go here to see a film.

Children play and have fun here.

2 Write a definition for the two missing words.

3 Look and read. Choose the correct words and write them on the lines. There is one example.

a station

a forest

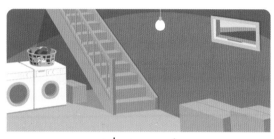

a basement

grass

a village

a lift

a roof

a hospital

Example

This is a quiet place to live in the countryside.

a village

Questions

1 People often go here when they aren't well.

2 This is on top of your house to keep it warm and dry.

3 People wait here to catch a train.

4 This machine takes you up and down a tall building.

5 This grows in fields and sheep love to eat it.

Movers Reading and Writing

1 Read and match. Draw the lines. There is one example.

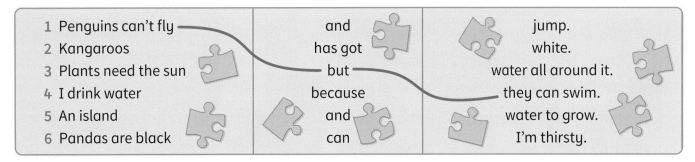

1 Penguins can't fly
2 Kangaroos
3 Plants need the sun
4 I drink water
5 An island
6 Pandas are black

and
has got
but
because
and
can

jump.
white.
water all around it.
they can swim.
water to grow.
I'm thirsty.

2 Read the text. Choose the right words and write them on the lines. There is one example.

Kangaroos

It isn't easy to see kangaroos (example): _____because_____ they only live in a country called Australia. They eat grass, but they don't need (1) _____ water.

Kangaroos are different from other animals because they cannot run or walk. They (2) _____. They (3) _____ one of the only animals in the world that moves around in this way.

Their two strong legs, huge feet and long tail help them jump. They can also (4) _____ very well.

Did you know that when kangaroos stand up, they are (5) _____ than a person?

Example: then (because) but

1 many   a   a lot of

2 hop   hops   hopping

3 is   are   was

4 swim   swam   swimming

5 tall   taller   more tall

Movers Speaking

1 **Look. Find the differences. Complete the sentences. There is one example.**

Example: The bed is pink in this picture, but in this one it's ___orange___ .

1 In this picture the girl has got brown hair, but here she has _____ .
2 The jacket is red, but this one's _____ .
3 Here you can see a dolphin, but here there's a _____ .
4 There's a cupboard behind the door, but here there's a _____ .
5 Here the girl is holding a book, but here she's got _____ .

2 **Look. Find the differences. Talk about the pictures.**

Movers Speaking

1 Look. Tell the story with your partner. Read and number. There is one example.

A dolphin helps

Example: The girl is crying. — `3`

The family are driving to the beach. ☐

A dolphin has got the ball. ☐

The children are playing with a ball. ☐

Mum is eating a sandwich. ☐

The girl is sitting on her dad's shoulders. ☐

The boy can't get the ball. ☐

Dad is taking a photo. ☐

The family are watching the dolphin. ☐

2 🎧 98 🐵 Look and listen. Then continue the story.

Picnic time by the river

Thanks and Acknowledgements

Authors' thanks

The authors and publishers acknowledge the following sources of copyright material and are grateful for the permissions granted. While every effort has been made, it has not always been possible to identify the sources of all the material used, or to trace all copyright holders. If any omissions are brought to our notice, we will be happy to include the appropriate acknowledgments on reprinting and in the next update to the digital edition, as applicable.

Key: U = Unit, R = Review, V= Values

General

Many thanks to everyone at Cambridge University Press and Assessment for their dedication and hard work, and in particular to: Liane Grainger and Lynn Townsend for supervising the whole project and guiding us calmly through the storms; Zara Hutchinson-Goncalves for her energy, enthusiasm and expertise. Thanks for doing such a great job.

We would also like to thank all our pupils and colleagues, past, present and future, at Star English academy in Murcia, especially Jim Kelly for his friendship and support throughout the years.

For the women who were my pillars of strength when I most needed it: Milagros Marin, Sara de Alba, Elia Navarro and Maricarmen Balsalobre. – CN

To Pablo and Carlota. This one's for you. Kid's Box's biggest fans. – MT

Photography

All the photos are sourced from Getty Images.

U0: chuckcollier/E+; **U1:** Morsa Images/E+; Ariel Skelley/DigitalVision; JGI/Jamie Grill; **U2:** Rosemary Calvert/Photodisc; Nazar Abbas Photography/Moment; Daniel Bosma/Moment; Canetti/iStock/Getty Images Plus; alabn/iStock/Getty Images Plus; Julien McRoberts; VectorPocket/iStock/Getty Images Plus; Francesco Riccardo Iacomino/Moment; photography by Sanchai Loongroong/Moment; ManuelVelasco/E+; Alex Levine/500px; Sydney James/DigitalVision; bombuscreative/DigitalVision Vectors; Cavan Images; **U3:** DigiPub/Moment; Jieophoto/iStock/Getty Images Plus; Wa Nity Canthra/EyeEm; Irina Cheremisinova/iStock/Getty Images Plus; Pakhnyushchyy/iStock/Getty Images Plus; asikkk/iStock/Getty Images Plus; Kyryl Gorlov/iStock/Getty Images Plus; Ninel Roshchina/iStock/Getty Images Plus; Lumi Images/Sveinn Baldvinsson; Jonathan Knowles/Stone; Matthias Kulka/The Image Bank; Stocktrek Images; McIninch/iStock/Getty Images Plus; **U4:** d3sign/Moment; Iryna Veklich/Moment; RichVintage/E+; Colors Hunter – Chasseur de Couleurs/Moment Open; M_a_y_a/E+; D. Sharon Pruitt Pink Sherbet Photography/Moment; Karen M. Romanko/Photodisc; Kei Uesugi/Stone; RBB/Moment; joSon/Stone; **U5:** Yoshiyoshi Hirokawa/DigitalVision; Tom Le Goff/Photodisc; stefanamer/iStock/Getty Images Plus; parinyabinsuk/iStock/Getty Images Plus; Weerameth Weerachotewong/EyeEm ; AaronAmat/iStock/Getty Images Plus; sdominick/iStock/Getty Images Plus; Photodjo/iStock/Getty Images Plus; yourstockbank/iStock/Getty Images Plus; LittleBee80/iStock/Getty Images Plus; vitapix/iStock/Getty Images Plus; Khosrork/iStock/Getty Images Plus; Suriya Silsaksom/EyeEm; Virojt Changyencham/Moment; Mint Images/Mint Images RF; clubfoto/iStock/Getty Images Plus; alkir/iStock/Getty Images Plus; SCIENCE PHOTO LIBRARY/Science Photo Library; Kiyoshi Hijiki/Moment; Jena Ardell/Moment; kuritafsheen/RooM; Anjelika Gretskaia/Moment; paci77/DigitalVision Vectors; LPETTET/DigitalVision Vectors; MIXA; Iryna Veklich/Moment; Burke/Triolo Productions/The Image Bank; BSIP; vitapix/E+; Jose Luis Pelaez Inc/DigitalVision; Kwanchai Chai-Udom/EyeEm; Science Photo Library; Rob Lewine; Raimund Koch/The Image Bank; fcafotodigital/E+; **U6:** Mint Images/Mint Images RF; yongyuan/E+; Images By Tang Ming Tung/Stone; JohnnyGreig/E+; gahsoon/E+; **U7:** IronHeart/Moment; Mike Hill/Stone; Simon McGill/Moment; Nimit Virdi/500px; Glowimages; Image Source; Lazareva/iStock/Getty Images Plus; Rüdiger Katterwe/EyeEm; USO/iStock/Getty Images Plus; Raimund Linke/The Image Bank; Gerard Soury/The Image Bank; JAH/iStock/Getty Images Plus; Fotosearch; SKapl/iStock/Getty Images Plus; SunRay BRI Cattery RU/iStock/Getty Images Plus; Nerthuz/iStock/Getty Images Plus; texcroc/E+; Hung_Chung_Chih/iStock/Getty Images Plus; goldhafen/E+; spxChrome/E+; Jonathan Fromager/EyeEm; Freder/E+; Martin Harvey/DigitalVision; amar pixler/500px Prime; Savushkin/E+; Claude LeTien/Moment; milehightraveler/E+; Steven Greenfield/500px; Trey Thomas/500px Prime; Glowimages; Stuart Westmorland/Corbis Documentary; jez_bennett/iStock/Getty Images Plus; **U8:** Marco Bottigelli/Moment; Danica Jovanov/iStock/Getty Images Plus; spanteldotru/E+; Bobbushphoto/iStock/Getty Images Plus; Os Tartarouchos/Moment; Peter Zelei Images/Moment; standret/iStock/Getty Images Plus; Thanapol Kuptanisakorn/EyeEm; Westend61; Moof/Image Source; George Doyle/Stockbyte; Andrea Evangelo-Giamou/EyeEm; ManoAfrica/E+; Trịnh Ngọc Đại/500Px Plus; Paul Souders/Stone; Rodrigo Echevarria/EyeEm; Ed Reschke/Stone; Pablo Perdomo/Moment; Peter Yates/500px; lindsay_imagery/E+; Lelia Valduga/Moment; gradyreese/E+; **R12:** Oscar Martín/Moment; Image Source; Michael Blann/Stone; studiocasper/E+; JGI/Tom Grill; fotoVoyager/iStock/Getty Images Plus; Working In Media/iStock/Getty Images Plus; allanswart/iStock/Getty Images Plus; alabn/iStock/Getty Images Plus; John Lawson, Belhaven/Moment Open; Westend61; Kevin Brine/iStock/Getty Images Plus; Simon McGill/Moment; scibak/E+; Pgiam/iStock/Getty Images Plus; Thomas M. Scheer/EyeEm; Emma Kim/Image Source; Image Source/Steve Prezant; Nastia11/iStock/Getty Images Plus; Morsa Images/DigitalVision; Roy Cheung/500px Prime; imaginima/iStock/Getty Images Plus; John Keeble/Moment; Nikola Ilic/E+; Maskot; monkeybusinessimages/iStock/Getty Images Plus; manley099/E+; DonNichols/E+; Wa Nity Canthra/EyeEm; Chiradech/iStock/Getty Images Plus; tiler84/iStock/Getty Images Plus; ManuelVelasco/E+; Sydney James/DigitalVision; **R34:** swetta/E+; baona/E+; Csondy/E+; shilh/iStock/Getty Images Plus; Barry Winiker/Photodisc; Glasshouse Images/The Image Bank Unreleased; Brian Keith Lorraine/Moment; photography by p. lubas/Moment; **R78:** Freder/iStock/Getty Images Plus; kertlis/E+; Colin Horn/Moment; sizsus/iStock/Getty Images Plus; GlobalP/iStock/Getty Images Plus; SEAN GLADWELL/Moment; anderm/iStock/Getty Images Plus; JulyKat/iStock/Getty Images Plus; apple2499/iStock/Getty Images Plus; mikroman6/Moment; Chris McLoughlin/Moment; KEHAN CHEN/Moment; Image Source; borchee/E+; Vivien.x.Li/Moment; swetta/E+; AlesVeluscek/E+; Daniel Rogers-Bromley/EyeEm; sebastian-julian/iStock/Getty Images Plus; GK Hart/Vikki Hart/DigitalVision; TanyaRozhnovskaya/iStock/Getty Images Plus; hadynyah/E+; Peter Gabriels/EyeEm; NYS444/iStock/Getty Images Plus; Photos by R A Kearton/Moment; WAS_/iStock/Getty Images Plus; shilh/iStock/Getty Images Plus; **V12:** Jakovo/iStock/Getty Images Plus; fstop123/E+; SolStock/E+; Hill Street Studios/DigitalVision; fanjianhua/Moment; **V34:** nature/iStock/Getty Images Plus; Patricia Marroquin/Moment; simon2579/DigitalVision Vectors; Carmen Martínez Torrón/Moment; **V56:** Comstock/Stockbyte; Productions/E+; Syldavia/iStock/Getty Images Plus; Lorado/E+; **V78:** Sasi Ponchaisang/EyeEm; Ronnie Kaufman/DigitalVision; SDI Productions/E+; lolostock/iStock/Getty Images Plus.

Illustrations

Antonio Cuesta (direct); Marek Jagucki (direct); Carol Herring, Leo Trinidad (Bright); Michael McCabe, Diego Diaz, Gustavo Berardo, Ilias Arahovitis (Beehive); Pronk Media Inc.

Cover illustration by Pronk Media Inc.

Audio

Audio production by Creative Listening.

Video

Video acknowledgements are in the Teacher Resources on Cambridge One.

Design and typeset

Blooberry Design

Additional authors

Katy Kelly: Lock's Sounds and spelling
Rebecca Legros: maths, geography, science and music sections
Monste Watkin: Exam Folders

Freelance editor

Wendy Cherry